Medieval World

CASTLES

SEAN SHEEHAN

A⁺

Smart Apple Media

First published in the UK by Franklin Watts
96 Leonard Street, London EC2A 4XD

Produced by Arcturus Publishing Ltd.
26/27 Bickels Yard, 151-153 Bermondsey Street, London SE1 3HA
Copyright © 2004 Arcturus Publishing Ltd.

Series concept: Alex Woolf
Editor: Clare Weaver
Designer: Chris Halls, Mind's Eye Design Ltd., Lewes
Illustrator: Peter Dennis
Picture researcher: Glass Onion Pictures

Published in the United States by Smart Apple Media
2140 Howard Drive West, North Mankato, MN 56003

Library of Congress Control Number: 2004104269

ISBN 1-58340-569-0

9 8 7 6 5 4 3 2 1

Picture Acknowledgements: The Art Archive, *cover*, 23, /Aarhus Kunstmuseum
Aarhus Denmark/Dagli Orti 4, /Ciano d'Enza Emilia Romagna Italy/Dagli Orti 6,
/JFB 14, /Biblioteca Nazionale Marciana Venice/Dagli Orti (A) 17, /Museo del
Baregello Florence/Dagli Orti 19, /Musee des Arts Decoratifs Paris/Dagli Orti (A)
20, /Jarrold Publishing 25, /University Library Heidelberg/Dagli Orti (A) 27;
English Heritage/HIP 13; National Archives 10; Topham Picturepoint 5, 29.

CONTENTS

Castles and the Medieval World   4

The Parts of a Castle   6

Types of Castles   8

Building a Castle   10

Keeping Out the Enemy   12

Castle Under Siege   14

Feudalism and Castles   16

Living in a Castle   18

Working in a Castle   20

Food and the Kitchen   22

Castle Luxuries   24

Entertainment and Leisure   26

Castle Fatigue   28

Timeline   30

Glossary and Further Information   31

Index   32

CASTLES AND THE MEDIEVAL WORLD

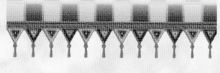

A modern painting of Rolf Gangr, leader of Viking pirates, on the coast of northern France at the start of the 10th century.

Castles first appeared in northern Europe in the 10th century A.D., in a period of time known as the early medieval age. Before the medieval period, the Roman empire had provided stability for much of Europe, with its good roads, trained armies, forts, and defensive walls. Beginning in the fifth century, however, the empire began to break up, and everything began to change. There were large migrations of people across Europe, from the east and from the far north. Vikings, from Norway, Sweden, and Denmark, settled in northern France and became known as Normans (the "Northmen"). There was also a dramatic expansion of Islam, and a Muslim empire developed across parts of the Mediterranean world. A king called Charlemagne, or Charles the Great, came to rule much of western Europe, but after he died in 814, his empire broke up.

By around 1000, most of western Europe had settled into a number of different kingdoms. These states were based around ruling families who saw their kingdoms as their own private property. The rulers wanted to protect their property and have soldiers ready and willing to fight for them. At the same time, they wanted a secure home in which to live and enjoy their wealth. This was the medieval world out of which castles first appeared and developed.

The history of the Normans explains why castles came to be built in England. In 1066, the Normans invaded England and, after defeating the ruling king, set about controlling their new kingdom. They needed to show their authority and crush rebellions that broke out across the country. In 1070, there was a general uprising in the north of England, as well as smaller ones in the south of the country. Danish ships arrived to support the rebels. It was this kind of military insecurity that prompted the Normans to build castles.

Castles were fortified country houses, and they were built throughout the medieval age, from the 10th to the 15th centuries. Wherever they were built, from northern Europe to the Middle East, they shared certain features that made them all recognizable as castles.

Built in southern Germany, Neuschwanstein Castle is what people like to imagine castles of the medieval age looked like.

Medieval Life
Only a tiny minority of people, the very rich, could afford to build and live in a castle. Most people spent their lives in the countryside, living off the land and working on a small farm for which they paid rent and taxes. Towns were just beginning to develop in the early medieval age. Most people could not read or write. A peasant farmer was unlikely to live beyond the age of 30, and the average height of a man was just over five feet (1.65 m); women were a little shorter.

THE PARTS OF A CASTLE

Dungeon

A castle keep was originally called a "donjon," an old French word. When the Normans first came to England, they transported a ready-made wooden donjon for their king. It was set up at Hastings, the town where the Norman king defeated the English ruler. Over time, the word "donjon" came to mean the room in the tower where prisoners were kept. Later, the word "dungeon" came to mean "prison," and because the donjon moved to below ground level in a castle, it came to mean an underground prison.

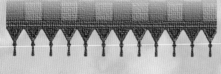

At the heart of a castle is its tower, also called a keep, usually round or square in shape. The number of levels within the keep would depend on its size, and the wealth of its owner, but one floor would make up the castle's main hall. The hall was the center of life in a castle. People would gather here to eat and be entertained. Other levels and rooms within the keep would be used for bedrooms, and while a separate kitchen would later be added, food was cooked out of doors to avoid the risk of fire in castles made of wood. In an emergency, the keep was a castle's last line of defense, for this is where people could lock themselves in and hold out against

The ruins of a real 10th-century castle in Italy bear little resemblance to people's romantic image of medieval castles.

The main parts of a castle: the keep, walls, bailey, gatehouse, and a moat.

an enemy for as long as possible. Usually, the castle's well would be below the keep so that there was always a source of water in the event of a siege.

A strong wall, now called a curtain wall, was built around the outside of the keep. At first, it was made of wood. Later, stone was used. The enclosed area between the inside of the wall and the keep is known as the bailey. As an open space, the bailey provided room for soldiers to gather. Since soldiers needed horses for transportation, the bailey also provided space for stables. Other outbuildings, for storing equipment and supplies, could also be built. Larger castles could have an additional, second wall built around the original one; this created two baileys, an outer and an inner one.

The gatehouse was a castle's front door, and since it was the place where an enemy might try to break in, it needed to be especially well protected. Many castles had a moat—a trench filled with water, or kept dry and sometimes planted with sharp stakes—around the outside of the walls. The gatehouse would face the only bridge over the water. By attaching the bridge to the gatehouse and making it possible to draw the bridge up or down, the resulting drawbridge formed a strong defense against enemies.

A Castle Keep

This is a description of a large castle's keep, or central tower. It was written in 1117 and refers to a wooden castle built some 75 years earlier:

"The first story was on the surface of the ground, where were cellars and granaries, and great boxes, tuns [containers], casks [barrels], and other domestic utensils. In the story above were the dwelling and common living room of the residents, in which were the larders [food storage], the rooms of the bakers and butlers, and the great chamber in which the lord and his lady slept."
(*From* The Medieval Castle, *Philip Warner*)

TYPES OF CASTLES

The earliest type of castle was built on a large mound of earth, which could be as high as a six-story house. Digging out earth for the mound created a ditch that could form the castle's moat. A wall of earth and timber formed a defensive barrier around the keep. The central mound was called a "motte" in French, from which the word "moat" comes, and this type of castle came to be known as the motte and bailey castle.

A motte and bailey castle.

Castle Motto
This Latin verse was written on a stone arch of Krak des Chevaliers:
"Sit tibi copia
Sit sapiencia
Formaque detur
Inquinat omnia sola
Superba si comitetur"

"Have richness,
have wisdom,
have beauty,
but beware of pride
which spoils all it comes into
contact with"
(*From* Crusader Castles,
Hugh Kennedy)

At the end of the 11th century, stone began to be used instead of wood and earth for both the keep and the castle walls. Around the same time, the first of six Crusades got under way. The Crusades set out to expel Muslims from land in the Middle East regarded as sacred to Christians. Crusaders traveled through what is now Turkey and the Middle East, and they saw a new style of stone fortifications. They were on a far grander and impressive scale than anything seen in Europe. There were long defensive walls, with towers sticking out from them at regular intervals, from which defenders could overlook an attacking force and prepare for their arrival. The fortified walls of Muslim castles and towns were also built to include areas of bare rock, even cliff edges, making such a castle far more difficult to attack. As the crusaders set about building their own castles in the Middle East, they were influenced by these Muslim designs.

Crusader castles led to the building of larger and more ambitious castles back in Europe. Massive gatehouses were constructed, and towers were added to castle walls. This new type of structure came to be called the concentric castle, because there was more than one surrounding wall. By the 13th century, when concentric castles were becoming common, some were being built without a keep. Instead, inside the outer wall, there was another wall connecting a series of towers. Even if an enemy broke through the outer wall, there was, in effect, a second castle securely defended and stored with provisions.

The Crusades also taught European rulers the military value of building more than one castle in a particular territory. With a group of castles, the soldiers inside them could then support one another. Any enemy that wanted to try and gain control and ownership of a territory would have to take on the combined force of a group of castles.

Krak des Chevaliers

The finest and most elaborate Crusader castle, Krak des Chevaliers, was first built in the Middle East, in what is now Syria, in the second half of the 12th century. It could hold up to 2,000 people and had two very strong stone walls surrounding it. The Muslim military leader, Saladin, decided in 1188 that the castle was too powerful to be captured. The walls and projecting towers were fitted with slits for archers to fire from and positioned in such a way as to cover most of the outside ground.

Krak des Chevaliers, in Syria, the greatest Crusader castle.

BUILDING A CASTLE

The Cost of Living

A mason earned four pennies a day [there were about 360 pennies to a dollar], a semi-skilled cutter of stone earned about half this, while an unskilled laborer was paid one penny a day. An ordinary knight earned about $30 a year, but an income of several hundred dollars a year was needed to run a castle. A large castle could cost more than $15,000 to build [about $4.5 million in present-day values].

The most important person in the building of a castle was the master mason. Partly an architect and partly an engineer, he would discuss building plans with the person who wanted a castle built. A building contract would often be drawn up between them, setting out the costs and what the builder was expected to do in return for the money being spent. The contract would be written twice on a single sheet of parchment, and then the sheet was cut along an indented line. Each party to the contract kept his own copy, which matched the other exactly, including the course of the wavy or zig-zag line along which the copies had been cut. This kind of contract was known as an indenture.

After agreeing on the kind of castle to be built, the master mason used a basic knowledge of geometry to work out the shape and proportions of the planned building. A quarry was needed, as close to the building site as possible, where square

An example of an indenture, showing clearly the zig-zag cut line.

An artist's impression of a master mason supervising work on a stone block for a castle keep; the keep can be seen in the background.

blocks of stone could be cut out of the ground. Axes and chisels of various sizes were used to cut the stone, and finer chisels and mallets were used to carve out decorative designs from cut stones. Mortar, needed to hold the stone together, was made by burning chalk or limestone in ovens specially prepared for the purpose. The burning produced quicklime, to which water and sand was added to make the mortar.

Carpenters, metal workers, and other masons all worked under the master mason. A smith was also needed to replace and sharpen the various building tools. Ladders, scaffolding, ramps, and pulley systems were all used in the building of a castle. Walls were mostly filled with rubble and mortar and finished with quality stone, called ashlar, which had been cut to size and smoothed carefully. In northern Europe, the building of a castle took place only during the warmer months of the year, and at the end of summer, walls were covered over to protect them from winter rains and frosts. Work would start again in spring. A large castle could take years to complete.

"License to Crenellate"

In England and France, a "license to crenellate" ("to fortify") needed to be granted by the king before a castle could be built. The following extract comes from a license issued by Henry IV of England in 1403: "License for the king's esquire James de Radeclif newly to enclose his manor-house of Radeclif, held of the king in-chief as of the duchy of Lancaster, with walls made of stone and lime [mortar] and within these to build a new hall with two towers similarly of stone and lime, and to crenellate the walls, hall, and towers thus made with battlements; and to hold the manor as a fortress." (*From* Castles in Medieval Society, *Charles Coulson*)

KEEPING OUT THE ENEMY

Grim Reality

This description of a battle for a castle provides a grim reminder of the reality of medieval warfare:

"One falls with gushing entrails [a body's insides], one with his throat cut, there a thigh is shattered by a staff, here brains are scattered with a club. One man's hand is shorn off with a sword, another forfeits [gives up] both knees to an axe. And still none draws back from the fight until the pitch [hot oil] from above causes them to step back. One groans as he breathes his last from a sword stroke in the face."
(*From* The Medieval Castle, *Philip Warner*)

A castle was built to withstand attack from an enemy. Any attack would have to cross the moat and break through the walls or the gatehouse to enter the castle. In order to strengthen the gatehouse area, strong towers known as barbicans were added. They would usually be part of the gatehouse wall but projecting forward so as to provide extra cover for defenders.

An artist's impression of soldiers defending a castle from attack.

Warkworth Castle, in the north of England, showing arrow loops and battlements.

In order to strengthen castle walls against the effect of battering rams, stone work was added to the bottom of walls. This made them thicker and gave them an outward slope. Large stones, dropped from above, could bounce off the slope and into the bodies and faces of enemy soldiers. Castle walls, especially above the gatehouse, had overhangs with holes built into them, known as machicolation. Castle defenders could easily drop stones or boiling oil onto the attacking soldiers through these holes.

Castle walls were also built with narrow openings, known as arrow loops, through which a defender could shoot. From the inside, the walls at the sides of the arrow loop opened widely so a bowman could stand comfortably. From the outside, however, narrow arrow loops were difficult to shoot at. The top of a castle wall had openings called crenels. The sections of wall in between were called merlons. These crenels and the much wider merlons formed a castle's battlements. From the battlements, bowmen could fire their arrows at an advancing enemy.

The inner side of battlements were usually left exposed to the castle interior, with a narrow walkway that was just wide enough to hold a few men. If an enemy did manage to climb the walls and clamber over the battlements, he was exposed to attack from inside the castle.

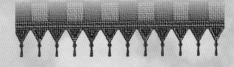

Chivalry

For knights and other nobles, war was seen as something brave and heroic. Both sides in a war shared similar ideas about winning glory and showing charity and loyalty. This heroic code of conduct was called chivalry, although it did not extend to the treatment of Muslims and Jews. Such non-Christians were usually regarded as inferior, people who did not deserve the normal rules of behavior. Knights, if they were defeated by their own kind, could expect to be ransomed rather than killed. Common soldiers, however, were expected to fight and die for their lords. Chivalry protected knights and nobles from the grim realities of war.

CASTLE UNDER SIEGE

Food for a Siege

A castle's ability to withstand a long siege depended on its supply of food and water, and a good supply of grain was essential if flour was to be available for the making of bread over a long period of time. Krak des Chevaliers, a Crusader castle, had ovens, huge jars for storing oil, hundreds of sacks of grain, and a windmill on one of its towers for making flour from the grain. With reliable wells to supply water, as well as large cisterns for collecting rainwater, a castle could withstand a siege for many months.

A siege was an attack on a castle that was prepared to defend itself. The enemy force would try to break through the castle walls using a variety of means. The stone walls, more difficult to set afire than the wooden walls of earlier castles, could sometimes be mined from underground. This was not possible if the walls were built on a foundation of natural rock or if the water in the moat could not be drained elsewhere. Soldiers could try to climb the walls with ladders or break through with a battering ram. Both sides fired arrows and stones with bows and slings. By the 12th century, the crossbow was being used. There were also various types of siege engines that could launch huge stones. Occasionally, dead horses or rats would be hurled into a castle in the hope of spreading disease. Moveable towers, built of wood, could be wheeled up to castle walls, but defenders were often ready for this. They dug concealed pits whose covering would give way and tip a tower when it moved forward.

A castle under siege, with an early form of cannon being used in the attack.

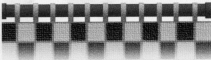

Siege machines being used to attack a castle that is well-protected with machicolations.

Mining a Castle

This account of the siege of a Crusader castle by Muslims in 1115 describes the mining of a castle:

"As soon as they got to the tower, they enlarged the tunnel in the wall of the tower, supported it on timbers, and began to carry out, a little at a time, the bits of stone produced by boring. . . . They then began to cut dry wood and stuff the tunnel with it. Early the next morning they set it on fire. We had just at that time put on our arms and marched under a great shower of stones and arrows to the trench in order to attack the castle as soon as the tower tumbled over. As soon as the fire began to have its effect, the layers of mortar between the stones of the wall began to fall. Then a crack was made. The crack became wider and wider, and the tower fell."
(From Crusader Castles, *Hugh Kennedy)*

If an attacking force could not break though the walls, they could always camp outside and wait patiently until the castle was starved into surrendering. Supplies and reinforcements were prevented from reaching the castle, and the defenders would have to try and manage on whatever supplies of food and arrows they already had. Injured soldiers needed to be treated, and infectious diseases such as dysentery were likely to spread in the cramped conditions of a castle under siege. At the same time, however, the attacking army also needed to be accommodated and fed, and this put pressure on its ability to maintain a long siege.

FEUDALISM AND CASTLES

In medieval Europe, a king or emperor held the most power in a country, but one person could not single-handedly control all of his territory. He needed the support of other wealthy and influential people, known as barons, whom he could trust and rely on for the supply of soldiers in the event of a war. Land would be given by a king to loyal barons, and these nobles, having received permission from the king, could build their own castles.

The class structure of medieval society.

King

Barons

Knights

Freemen

Peasants

Knights were a special class of soldiers who were obliged to serve their king or baron in times of war. In the early medieval period, knights often lived in the castles of nobles and formed the garrison—a body of soldiers ready to fight and defend the castle. Over time, many knights became wealthy lords, especially as a result of the Crusades, and were no longer obliged to fight. Instead, knights could now pay money to their king or baron, and this system, known as scutage, allowed many knights to live on their own land. As a result, a castle's garrison often came to be made up of soldiers and less wealthy knights who hired themselves out to lords.

The relationship between kings, barons, and lords was an important part of the medieval system. It was based on the exchange of land in return for service, which usually included military service. The vassal, the person providing service, swore loyalty to his ruler and offered his services in return for the land he was given. This became a ceremonial occasion, known as homage, and took place in the chapel of a castle or in a cathedral.

Peasants lived on, and farmed, the land that belonged to the nobles. The peasants had few rights and, after handing over a percentage of the produce they grew to the nobility, had barely enough to keep themselves alive. Their work allowed the nobles to enjoy privileged lives in their castles, and in return, the peasants were allowed to live on sections of the land. Serfs were a class of peasants who were the most poorly treated. They were little better than slaves and could be bought or sold like a piece of property.

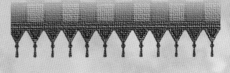

Peasants' Revolts

It was difficult for peasants to resist the power of soldiers who could ride out from a castle armed with their weapons, but there were still outbreaks of rebellion. In the 14th century, there were revolts in northern France that led to the burning of castles, and in 1381, peasants rebelled in England and took control of London for a brief period. They destroyed the castle of the king's uncle, and the king, Richard II, seemed to agree to their demands for justice. Their leader, Wat Tyler, made the mistake of trusting the king and was murdered as a result.

This 14th-century illustration shows a homage ceremony, or perhaps a king in the act of making someone a knight.

LIVING IN A CASTLE

Keeping Clean
Private baths were only for the wealthy, and a well-provided castle would have had its own bathtub, made of wood and lined with canvas. A handle at each end made it easy to move.

Castles, all of which were privately owned, were far more than military buildings. Although a king or high-ranking baron would spend most of his time traveling around the country, many castles were homes where a lord and his family lived and passed most of their time. Naturally, they would try to make their home as comfortable and attractive as possible. Bright colors were used to paint the inside and outside of castles, and care was taken in their upkeep. Henry III of England ordered the rainwater spouts on the Tower of London to be lengthened so that water marks would not stain the freshly painted, gleaming white walls.

An artist's impression of various activities inside a medieval castle.

The hall, in an early medieval castle, had a hole in the roof for smoke to escape through, and there was little other ventilation. Herbs might be scattered over the floor, and on the straw used as mattresses, to sweeten the air inside the castle.

The fireplace and tallow candles were the main sources of light. As the medieval age progressed, improvements were made to the living style of castle residents. The use of stone made it possible to build fireplaces into the wall and to add chimneys. The original keep of an old castle was often inadequate for living quarters, and new rooms could be built, sometimes surrounding a central courtyard. The basic division between the hall, with its fireplace, and a chamber for sleeping could be extended into groups of rooms, depending on the wealth of the castle owner.

Castle Rooms

These two accounts of castle rooms, drawn up in 1340 for two castles in England, give some idea of the living space available to the residents of a castle:

"The castle is well built, walled and crenellated, and has a stone tower and a moat. There are therein a great hall, two chambers, two chapels, a kitchen, and a bakery of stone; a gatehouse with a chamber, underneath which is a drawbridge."

"The castle is well walled and within are a hall, four chambers, a chapel, a kitchen, two stables, a grange [barn] for hay, a prison-house, a chamber for the gatekeeper, and a drawbridge with iron chains."
(*From* Castles in Medieval Society, *Charles Coulson*)

The wooden chest of a nobleman, from the early 15th century, decorated with scenes from the Crusades.

Furniture was a luxury in the medieval age, even for the wealthy few who lived in their own castle. There were beds, but chairs were uncommon, and an average-sized castle would possess very few. The most important person at any meeting always had the use of a chair—this is the origin of the term "chairperson." The basic item of furniture was a chest, where clothes and valuables, such as metal tableware, could be stored. Nobles who moved around the country, staying in their different castles, traveled with their chests.

WORKING IN A CASTLE

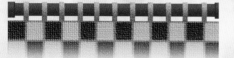

Paying Wages
The following accounts are for Chirk Castle in Wales at the end of the 13th century, and they refer to the wages bill for one year. A shilling (s), made up of 12 pennies (d), was roughly equivalent to today's dime, but it was worth much more in the Middle Ages.
"And in wages of the porter of the Castle for the same time 60s 10d taken by the day 2d.
And in wages of one park-keeper for the same time 30s 5d taken by the day 1d.
And in salary of one Chaplain for celebrating in the Castle for the year 53s 4d."
(*From* The Medieval Castle, *Philip Warner*)

Depending on its size, a castle was home to a number of people. If the castle owner was a king or an important baron, owning lots of land and homes, much time was spent traveling around from one castle to another. An official called a castellan, or constable, was appointed to be in charge of the castle while the king or baron was absent. Other barons and lords lived full-time in their castles, along with their wives and children, with various attendants and workers to service their needs.

In times of peace, a castle's garrison might consist of only a few soldiers, but knights and more soldiers could always be called upon when necessary. When traveling from one castle to another, a king or baron needed bodyguards, and servants were essential to attend to their needs while staying in a castle.

A painting showing ladies-in-waiting carrying out their work in a medieval setting.

A garrison made a castle seeem like a police station, but other people working in a castle made it seem more like a town hall. Officials called sheriffs could use a castle as their base, collecting payments from peasants and applying laws. Records needed to be kept, and clerks who could read and write were required for this purpose. The clergy were among the few who were literate, and clerks were often church officials who worked under the chaplain, the priest in charge of a castle's chapel.

Your Job is Your Name

A "villein" was the medieval term for a humble peasant, and being someone with no power or influence, such a person counted for little and could be blamed for anything. Over time, the word came to mean a low-born person who could not be trusted—hence the word "villain." Other occupations were the basis for a person's surname:

Smith: the name of a metalworker, a smith

Bowyer: a specialist in the making of bows

Cooper: someone in charge of the casks that stored beer and wine

Constable: a high-ranking official with important powers

Granger: official in charge of the barn or grange that stored grain

Salter: a specialist in the production of salt

Chamberlain: official in charge of the household, including the rooms, or chambers, of a king or baron

Butler: from "bottler," in charge of the wine cellar

An artist's impression of an armorer at work in a castle.

Servants and a blacksmith were needed to tend the horses, and an armorer carried out repairs to weapons and armor. Carpenters were needed for a variety of jobs, from making a soup bowl to a bed. There were cooks and servants called trenchermen, who carried and served food at the table. Ladies-in-waiting lived in a castle as the personal attendants of a noble family. There were also laundresses, bakers, and brewers of beer.

FOOD AND THE KITCHEN

Keeping Food Tasty

Preserving food, especially over winter when fresh produce was not so readily available, was very important in the medieval age. Meats, butter, cheese, and fish were all heavily salted for this reason. Castles had their own gardens to grow herbs for the purpose of adding flavor to the taste of vegetables, because spices were too expensive for most people in western Europe. Sugar was so rare that it was kept locked up in a castle, and honey was used as a sweetener. Food was also colored to make it more attractive; for example, by boiling mint or parsley for a green effect, or extracting a red dye from sandalwood.

Producing food was a vital matter in the medieval age because it was not something that could be taken for granted. Indeed, the power and influence of those who built castles partly depended on their ability to provide food for their knights, attendants, and servants. The title "lord" comes from an old English word "hláford," which meant "keeper of bread."

Grain, usually made into bread, was the basis of the medieval diet, although the kind of bread eaten depended on a person's place in the feudal order. Wastrel, white bread from grain that was finely sieved and ground, was reserved for a lord and his family; poorer people ate brown bread made from bran or rye. Breads left to grow hard for a few days after baking were used as disposable plates called trenchers. Forks were

Kitchen staff busy at work preparing and cooking food in a castle.

The nobility in a 15th-century French castle are served food, with live music provided in the background.

Roasted Peacock
The earliest cookbooks appeared in Denmark in the 13th century, and over the following two centuries, recipes began to appear in the rest of northern Europe: "Take a peacock, break its neck, and cut its throat, and flay it [strip off], skin and feathers together, with the head still attached to the skin of the neck, and keep the skin and the feathers whole together. . . . And when it is roasted, take it off and let it cool, and then wind the skin with the feathers and the tail about the body, and serve it as if the bird were still alive." (*From* The Pimlico Encyclopedia of the Middle Ages, *Norman F. Cantor*)

not used, and food was eaten by hand or with spoons after it had been cut up with a knife. People carried their own knives, which were kept in special cases or carried in a sheath. The drinking of wine was reserved for the wealthy, while ordinary people consumed beer or, by fermenting honey and water, a drink called mead.

The nobility in a castle ate far better food than that available to peasants working in the fields. Poor people could not afford to eat meat on a regular basis, but beef, mutton, and a variety of wild birds provided meat dishes for lords and their families. The kitchen, a vital part of any castle, was kept separate from the main hall, but it later came to be connected by a passageway. A kitchen might use an open fire, or an oven could be set into a wall. A large castle would have a separate bakery, for the daily production of fresh bread, as well as a pantry for storing food. Kitchen equipment, such as a cooking pot, was made of iron, copper, or bronze, while jugs for holding wine and other liquids were made of pottery.

CASTLE LUXURIES

Showing Off

In this French medieval account of an argument about dress, Master Robert de Sorbon accuses his friend of showing off his wealth: "'You certainly deserve a reprimand [a telling-off] for being more richly dressed than the king, since you are wearing a fur-trimmed mantle of fine green cloth, and he wears no such thing.' 'Master Robert,' I answered, 'I am, if you'll allow me to say so, doing nothing worthy of blame in wearing green cloth and fur, for I inherited the right to such dress from my father and mother. But you, on the other hand, are much to blame, for though both your parents were commoners, you have abandoned their style of dress, and now wear finer woolen cloth than the king himself.'" (*From* Medieval Civilization, *Jacques Le Goff*)

Head coverings and hats were popular in the medieval age, and the nobility displayed the more fashionable styles.

The medieval age covered many centuries, and over time there were improvements in the nature of castle life. In the 10th century, there was little commercial trade between the different areas of Europe. By the 14th century, trade links across Europe and the Mediterranean were well established. The benefits of this trade were available not to the majority of people who farmed the land, but to wealthy families who lived in castles. The nobility were able to purchase goods and luxuries that were previously difficult to obtain.

The rich owners of castles displayed their wealth in the clothes they wore, using materials such as silk, satin, and mink. Damask, a rich silk fabric woven with elaborate designs and

often in a variety of colors, got its name from the city of Damascus, in the Middle East. The Crusades had opened up to Europeans a whole range of luxury goods, including tapestries, carpets, and spices, as well as fine silk fabrics. From Russia came a variety of furs that were used to line clothes and bed covers, providing extra warmth in the cold and drafty rooms of a castle. In France and Holland, a plant called madder was used to make a dye that could add color to cloth and distinguish the owner of such clothes. The growing of flax made linen clothing more important, and shirts and underwear began to be worn.

The Fur Trade
Peasants in Russia and Finland captured and skinned minks, otters, foxes, squirrels, beavers, martens, stoats, bears, and other animals. The skins ended up in markets in eastern Europe. From there, they were sold to other merchants in western Europe. The final stage was the making of garments from the furs, and these were then sold to wealthy people who could afford them. The more pelts, or animal skins, that went into a piece of clothing, the higher the social status of the wearer. A full fur coat worn by a French king was said to come from more than 350 pelts.

Colorful carpets and embroidered fabrics on chairs were luxury items available to the wealthy owners of castles.

As castles became bigger, extra rooms were added, and chambers could be provided for guests. Tapestries could be hung from a wall, acting as a screen and dividing bedrooms, and ceilings might be painted with a design or a picture. The greatest wealth of a castle was likely to be in the chapel, in the form of vestments using expensive materials, and plates and church ornaments made from precious metals such as gold and silver.

ENTERTAINMENT AND LEISURE

Games and Gambling in Castles

The game of chess, which had spread to the Islamic world from India, was discovered by the crusaders in the Middle East and brought back to Europe. Card games were also borrowed from Muslim culture, as well as the board game backgammon, which had been developed in the Middle East. Gambling, forbidden by Islam, was enjoyed in non-Muslim parts of the medieval world, and bets were placed on the outcome of a tournament or the roll of dice.

A castle was a home, and when military matters could be put to one side, it was a place where people enjoyed themselves when not at work. Children played games that would be recognized today as leapfrog, blind man's bluff, and tug-of-war. A variety of ball games were played by young people, but although they resembled games such as tennis and hockey, rubber had not yet been discovered, so balls did not bounce.

In the medieval age, there were professional entertainers who would visit a castle to play music and sing ballads. Music was popular, and it was danced to, as well as played as an accompaniment to the telling of stories. Minstrels, troubadours, and jongleurs were names for different types of

In the 13th century, jousts became a popular form of entertainment. Blunted weapons were frequently used, to avoid serious injuries.

A 14th-century German manuscript showing Emperor Otto IV playing chess with a woman.

entertainers who sang and played musical instruments. Feasts were an important part of medieval social life, and musicians would be hired for a castle banquet celebrating an official event or a holiday occasion.

The importance of war in medieval life meant that it affected forms of entertainment and leisure. Part of the popularity of the game of chess in medieval times was due to its military character—"checkmate" derives from the Arabic "shah mat," meaning "the king is dead." In the course of time, the terms "castle," "castling," and "knight" were added to the language of the game. Tournaments and jousts, where mounted and armed knights engaged each other on horseback, were a combination of entertainment, sport, and military training.

For peasants, hunting was a practical activity intended to produce a meal on the table, but for the nobility, hunting for wild game and birds combined sport with military training. It allowed lords and knights to practice using various weapons and skills, and castles would often be close to a forested area that was the private property of the castle owner. In this way, part of a castle estate became a private game park for the rich to hunt boars and stags. Falcons and hawks were also trained to seize smaller birds, and this sport became known as falconry. A special building in a castle, called a mew, was used to keep a falcon.

A Castle to Enjoy
This 12th-century description of a castle combines military aspects with the mention of scenic features that were designed to be enjoyed in times of leisure:
"It is excellently well defended by turrets and bulwarks, and is situated on the summit of a hill, extending on the western side towards the sea-port, having on the north and south a fine fishpond hard by its wall, as conspicuous for its grand appearance as for the depth of its waters. On the same side is a beautiful orchard, bounded by a vineyard and elsewhere by a wood, remarkable for its projecting rocks and by the height of its hazel trees."
(From Castles in Medieval Society, *Charles Coulson*)

CASTLE FATIGUE

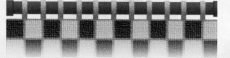

Romantic Castles
These lines from a 14th-century poem describe the kind of fairy-tale castle that still appeals to people's imagination: "Further in he saw the hall rising high, with towers all about, whose pinnacles rose high aloft, with carven tops cunningly wrought. On the tower roofs his eye picked out many white chimneys that gleamed like chalk cliffs in the sunlight. And there were so many pinnacles, gaily painted, scattered about everywhere and climbing one above another among the embrasures [openings] of the castle, that it looked as though it were cut out of paper."
(*From* Sir Gawain and the Green Knight)

The first cannons were simple, often ineffective devices, but by the late 15th century, improvements had turned them into important weapons for attacking castles.

Before the use of gunpowder, most means of attacking a castle relied on the muscle-power of soldiers. Gunpowder changed this because it released energy that could drive heavy objects, such as cannon balls, against a target. It could do serious damage without relying on the physical strength of large numbers of men.

Another important technological development towards the end of the medieval age was the ability to melt iron ore in a blast furnace. The liquid iron was poured into molds of a particular size and shape, and in this way, iron cannons could be manufactured. By using the explosive power of gunpowder,

cannons could direct and smash balls of cut stone against the walls of a castle. By delivering a force greater than any previous engine of war, gunpowder and cannons signaled the end of the age of castle building.

The new technology, however, was also available to the defenders of a castle, and castle building did not suddenly come to an end. Early cannons were difficult to use and not very mobile, and hand-held cannon guns were used by soldiers defending castles. Gunports for the new weapons were cut low into the walls so as to aim them directly at an attacking force. Arrow and crossbow loops were adjusted to handle hand cannons, and vents were added to carry away the smoke caused by the exploding gunpowder.

Gunpowder and the cannon, however, meant that castles could be successfully attacked without having to resort to long and costly sieges. In 1453, Turkish forces broke through the mighty fortifications of Constantinople using cannon guns to good effect. By the 16th century, castles were of military importance in only a few parts of Europe; Austria, for example, which was under threat from the advancing Turks. Castles in other areas were being converted into military forts and barracks, or were turned into grand homes. The idea of a castle as a fortified house, which needed to be defended against a possible attack, was becoming an idea of the past. The medieval age was over.

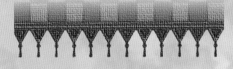

Fairy-Tale Castles

Centuries after the medieval age, castle building was resurrected. This time, however, castles were built as romantic reminders of a past age. They were fairy-tale castles, like the castle of Neuschwanstein, built in Germany towards the end of the 19th century, which inspired the Walt Disney logo. Another example, Castle Coch, in Wales, was built using the plans of a 13th-century castle that once stood on the same site. Medieval castles still hold great appeal, and people visit restored and rebuilt castles across Europe and in parts of the Middle East.

Castle Coch, built around the same time as Neuschwanstein Castle (see page 5), is a far more realistic example of what a medieval castle actually looked like.

TIMELINE

476   The last Roman emperor loses power to tribes invading western Europe.

711–1250   Years in which most of Spain is held by Muslim rulers.

814   The death of Charlemagne, a king whose empire included large parts of the Roman empire.

1066   Norman forces invade England and castles are built to secure their authority.

1070   A rebellion in the north of England against Norman authority.

1095–99   The First Crusade, a successful one that included the capture of Jerusalem.

1142–1271   Krak des Chevaliers, a very strong castle in the Middle East, is held by crusaders.

1147–49   The Second Crusade, a failure.

1188   Saladin, leader of the Muslims, gives up an attempt to capture the Crusader castle Krak des Chevaliers.

1189–92   The Third Crusade, with victories for both Christian and Muslim armies.

1202–04   The Fourth Crusade, a failure.

1220   From around this time, glass windows are made for castles.

1250   Castles with more than one stone wall, concentric castles, begin to be built.

1320   The first cannon produced in Europe.

1326   The first picture of a cannon appears in England.

1350   Cannons used regularly in castle sieges.

1381   The Peasants' Revolt in England.

1400   Smiths begin mixing the ingredients of gunpowder in water to produce a fine powder that is easier to use than earlier forms of gunpowder.

1453   Turkish forces successfully attack the strong fortifications of Constantinople using cannons.

1500   Most castles no longer function as fortified homes, except in some parts of Europe under threat from Muslim forces.

1869   Building work starts on Neuschwanstein Castle in Germany, in the style of a medieval castle.

1875   Castle Coch, in Wales, is built in a medieval style.

arrow loops Narrow openings in a castle wall through which defenders could shoot.

bailey The enclosed area of a castle, between the walls and the keep.

barbican A defensive tower built into a castle wall near the gateway.

baron A high-ranking lord who held land from a king in return for service.

battering rams Heavy beams of wood used for trying to break through castle walls.

battlements The top part of castle walls, consisting of crenels and merlons.

bulwarks A defensive wall, often made of earth.

cannon A large heavy gun.

castellan The person in charge of a castle.

catapult A machine for hurling large rocks at castle walls.

chaplain A religious person in charge of a castle's church.

constable Like a castellan, a person placed in charge of a castle.

crenel The gap between merlons at the top of a castle wall.

crenellate To make crenels, meaning to fortify a wall against the threat of attack.

Crusades A series of military expeditions with the aim of breaking Muslim control over what was seen as Christian Holy Land in the Middle East.

curtain wall The outer wall of a castle.

feudalism The medieval system by which a vassal held land from a superior in exchange for a service.

fortifications Defensive parts strengthened to resist attack.

garrison A body of soldiers ready to fight and defend a castle.

Holy Land A region of the Middle East, including Jerusalem, held sacred by Christians and Muslims.

homage A ceremonial occasion in the medieval age when a vassal swore loyalty to his ruler and offered his services in return for the land he was given.

indented A zig-zag line dividing two identical parts of a medieval document.

indenture A contract between two people.

jousts A competition between two knights who try to knock one another off the horses they are riding towards each other on.

keep The main tower of a castle.

knight A noble-born medieval soldier on horseback.

lord In the medieval age, a master or ruler over other people.

machicolation The part at the top of a castle wall with holes for dropping stones or hot oil down onto an enemy.

mallets Hammers made out of wood.

mason A person who builds using stone.

master mason The chief mason, in overall charge of the building of a castle.

mead An alcoholic drink made from fermented honey and water.

medieval age The period of European history between the fall of the Roman empire in 476 and the fall of Constantinople in 1453.

merlons The solid part between the gaps, the crenels, at the top of a castle wall.

Middle East The area covered by the land between Egypt and Iran.

migration A movement of people from one country to another country.

minstrel A medieval musician and singer.

moat A deep ditch around a castle, filled with water or sometimes kept dry.

mortar A mix of lime, sand, and water used for joining stones together.

motte A large mound on which the early form of castles was built.

nobles A landowning class in Europe in the medieval age.

Normans The descendants of Vikings who settled in northern France and went on to conquer England.

peasants People who worked on a lord's land in return for a small plot of land to grow food for themselves.

pinnacles The very top of a turret, shaped like a pyramid.

pulley system A system for lifting heavy weights using rope and a wheel.

Roman empire The control of Europe and part of the Middle East under the authority of Rome between 31 B.C. and A.D. 476.

rubble Rough pieces of stone of no fixed shape or size.

siege An attack on a castle, by surrounding it and preventing supplies and reinforcements from reaching it in the expectation that it will eventually surrender.

smith A worker in metal.

tallow candles Candles made from animal fat.

tournament A medieval entertainment involving jousts.

trenchermen Servants in the medieval age who carried and served food at the table.

troubadour A singer or poet of the medieval age.

turret A small tower on a castle wall.

vassal A holder of land on the condition of offering a service in return for the land.

vent A special opening that lets out smoke or air from a confined space.

wastrel A fine kind of bread in the medieval age

RECOMMENDED READING

Gravett, Christopher. *Castle*. New York: DK Publishing, 2000.

Langley, Andrew. *Medieval Life*. New York: DK Publishing, 2000.

Macaulay, David. *Castle*. New York: Houghton Mifflin, 1983.

Nardo, Don. *Medieval Castle*. New York: Gale Group, 1997.

RECOMMENDED WEB SITES

http://www.castles.org

http://www.castlesontheweb.com

http://www.sirclisto.com

INDEX

A

armorer 21
arrow loops 13

B

bailey 7
barbican 12
barons 16, 17, 18, 20
battering rams 13, 14
battlements 11, 13
bowman 13

C

cannon 14, 28, 29
Castle Coch 29
chaplain 20, 21
concentric castle 9
constable 20, 21
contract 10
crenels 13
Crusades 8, 9, 16
curtain wall 7

D

drawbridge 7, 19
dungeon 6

E

entertainment 26

F

feudalism 16

food 14, 15, 22
fortifications 8, 29
furniture 19

G

garrison 16, 20, 21
gatehouse 7, 9, 12, 13
gunpowder 28, 29

H

hall 6, 19, 23
homage 17

I

indenture 10

J

jousts 27

K

keep 6, 8, 19
kitchen 6, 19, 22, 23
knight 10, 13, 16, 27
Krak des Chevaliers 8, 9, 14

L

lord 7, 17, 18, 27

M

machicolation 13
mason 10
merlons 13

moat 7, 8, 12, 14, 19
motte and bailey castle 8
Muslims 4, 8, 9, 13, 15, 26

N

Neuschwanstein Castle 5, 29
nobles 13, 16, 19
Normans 4, 5

P

peasant 6, 16, 17, 21, 27

R

Roman empire 4
rubble 11

S

Saladin 9
siege 7, 14, 15
soldiers 7, 13, 14, 15, 17

T

tournaments 27
towers 9, 11, 12, 15, 19
trenchers 22

V

Vikings 4